T

D1263941

DAILY LIFE

Slaves on a Southern Plantation

Debbie Levy

KIDHAVEN
PRESS™

THOMSON
———— ✦ ————
GALE

San Diego • Detroit • New York • San Francisco • Cleveland
New Haven, Conn. • Waterville, Maine • London • Munich

© 2004 by KidHaven Press. KidHaven Press is an imprint of The Gale Group, Inc., a division of Thomson Learning, Inc.

KidHaven™ and Thomson Learning™ are trademarks used herein under license.

For more information, contact
KidHaven Press
27500 Drake Rd.
Farmington Hills, MI 48331-3535
Or you can visit our Internet site at http://www.gale.com

LIBRARY OF CONGRESS CATALOGING-IN-PUBLICATION DATA

Levy, Debbie, 1951–
  Slaves on a Southern Plantation / by Debbie Levy.
    p. cm. — (Daily Life)
Summary: Discusses the daily life of slaves on southern plantations including home life, family, work, and treatment by slave owners and society.
Includes bibliographical references and index.
  ISBN 0-7377-1827-7 (alk. paper)
1. Slaves—United States—Biography—Juvenile literature. 2. Slavery—United States—History—Juvenile literature. [1. Slaves. 2. Slavery.] I. Title. II. Series.

Printed in the United States of America

Contents

CHAPTER ONE

Working the Fields

S lavery in the United States started before 1700. That was when slave traders began capturing black people—men, women, and children—in their home countries in Africa. The traders shipped Africans across the Atlantic Ocean. In the American colonies, Africans were sold to whites and forced to work as slaves, without pay and without a say in their own lives. The slaves' children born in the United States were also enslaved, as were their grandchildren and great-grandchildren. Any baby born to a slave mother was considered a slave.

Slavery continued for more than 150 years, until the end of the Civil War in 1865. At first, slavery existed in all parts of the United States. Before long, however, it was limited to the South. There, farmers needed many workers to raise crops such as cotton, tobacco, rice, and sugarcane. Hiring and paying farmhands was expensive. The farmers could make more money if they had workers whom they did not have to pay. Slaves became the solution to the farmers' economic problem. They were especially important to owners of very large farms, known as **plantations**.

Life of Work

Robbed of the freedom to choose their lives, plantation slaves were forced into lives of work. Seasons and crops shaped their long days of labor. Their **masters**, or the slaves' owners, decided when and how they worked, what they wore, and what they ate. Plantation slaves did everything from plowing fields to building houses to cooking meals to tending children. The great majority, however, worked as **field hands**, toiling in the dirt to raise their masters' crops.

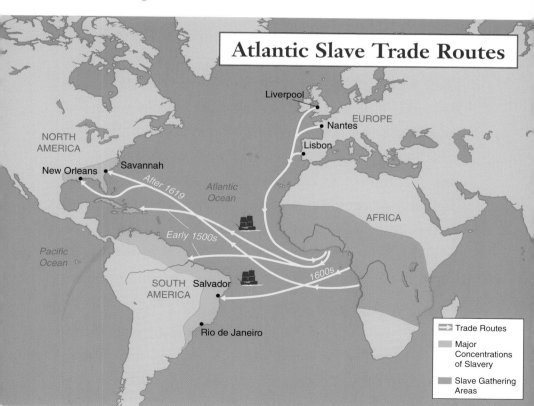

Atlantic Slave Trade Routes

Liverpool

EUROPE
Nantes

Lisbon

NORTH AMERICA

New Orleans   Savannah

After 1619

Atlantic Ocean

AFRICA

Pacific Ocean

Early 1500s

SOUTH   Salvador
AMERICA

1600s

Rio de Janeiro

Trade Routes

Major Concentrations of Slavery

Slave Gathering Areas

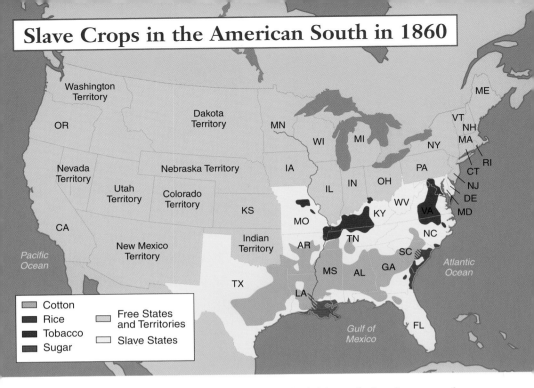

Slave Crops in the American South in 1860

Legend:
- Cotton
- Rice
- Tobacco
- Sugar
- Free States and Territories
- Slave States

Every day but Sunday, the field hands had to awaken before sunrise. There were no alarm clocks, but the slaves knew when it was time to get up. "At the earliest dawn of day, and frequently before that time, the laborers were roused from their sleep by the blowing of the horn," [1] recalled James Williams, who was a slave on an Alabama cotton plantation. Other plantation owners used bells, bugles, and pounding on doors with fists to welcome their workers to another day. "Bells and horns!" said Charley Williams, who was a slave in Louisiana. "Bells for this and horns for that!" [2]

Hours in the Field

On a large plantation, more than two hundred slaves might be called to the fields this way. As they hurried from their cabins, they might swallow a quick cold breakfast, called the "morning's bit" by some. But many slaves were too exhausted from the previous day's work to eat, and they could not manage to trade even a few minutes of sleep for a bite of food.

The field hands gathered to receive their orders from the **overseer**, the white man who supervised the slaves.

Slaves who worked as field hands awoke before sunrise to toil in their masters' fields.

Drivers, slaves chosen to lead groups of field hands, organized the hands to carry out the day's instructions. In the fields, drivers watched the other slaves and prodded them to work harder.

Around noon, the hands were allowed a break. Sometimes they had to stay in the field and eat from a bucket they had packed. Sometimes they were sent back to their cabins to eat, or told to gather at outdoor tables near the kitchen. After the midday meal, slaves were sent back to work. Often, they labored in the fields until dark. During the long days of summer, their workday could last sixteen hours, from four o'clock in the morning until eight o'clock at night.

Even then, field hands rarely relaxed. They had to cook their suppers, mend their clothes, and clean their cabins. Besides these personal tasks, slaves were called on to perform more work for their owners in the evenings. Sometimes, men were sent out to burn brush after dark. Women had to spin and weave cotton into cloth at night. Only after they cooked and ate supper, cleaned their cabins and clothes, and did whatever extra work their owners assigned them, did the field hands have time to sleep. And before too many hours passed, they would be summoned back to work.

Dirty Work

Farm labor was dirty and tedious. Jobs included planting seeds or seedlings, weeding and hoeing plants as they grew, and harvesting, or picking, mature crops. The details of the work depended on the crop. To grow cotton, for example, the slaves had to plow the land deeply in the

Working in the fields was dirty and tedious work,
particularly for crops like cotton.

early spring. Then, around the first of April, they planted
cottonseeds in the rows, or furrows, they had plowed.
Next came months of hoeing and plowing to protect the
growing cotton plants from weeds. By late August or
early September the cotton was ready for picking.

Harvest meant nonstop work, with little sleep and
no free time, for slaves. Plantation owners wanted to get
as much cotton picked and sold to cotton merchants as
soon as possible. They pushed their slaves to work even
more than usual. "The daily task of each able-bodied
slave during the cotton picking season was 250 pounds

or more," wrote Louis Hughes, who was a slave on a Mississippi plantation, "and all those who did not come up to the required amount would get a whipping." To urge the field hands on, the overseer sometimes arranged a contest. The slaves were divided into teams, and the team that produced the most during the contest was declared the winner. Hughes wrote: "They would all work like good fellows for the prize, which was a tin cup of sugar for each slave on the winning side."[3]

The harvest season lasted for months, into December or January. The slaves picked cotton in all kinds of weather. "The times I hated most," remembered Mary Reynolds, who was a slave in Louisiana, "was pickin' cotton when the frost was on the bolls. My hands git sore and crack open and bleed."[4]

Children in the Fields

Mary Reynolds was a young girl when she had to pick cotton until her hands bled. As soon as they were eight to twelve years old, children joined men and women in the fields. Toddlers might be allowed to play during the workday, under the supervision of an older woman slave or an older child. But even young children who were too small to hold a hoe had field jobs. They gathered brush and stacked it in piles when the older slaves were clearing land. They cleaned yards and weeded vegetable beds. They also kept watch in the fields keeping the bugs from destroying the crops: "My first employment was that of a scarecrow in the corn fields," wrote John Andrew Jackson of South Carolina. "I was driven into the field at the earliest dawn of day, and I did not leave the field till sunset." [5]

"Work, Work, Work"

During the coldest winter months the fields lay fallow. No crops were planted, tended, or harvested on the plantation. Still, the field hands were not idle. "In the winter I went to the woods with the menfolks to get wood or sap

A slave boy (right) cuts sugarcane as his owner watches. At the age of eight, most slave children went to work in the fields.

from the trees to make turpentine and tar," said Mingo White of Alabama. "We made charcoal to run the blacksmith shop with."[6] Slave owners also ordered their slaves to clear fields, fix tools, repair and clean barns, mend fences, and make other repairs.

And then, the seasons turned. Early spring came around again. The plantation's cycle of plowing, planting, tending, and harvesting started anew. For many people springtime is a season for new beginnings and change. But for the slaves, "the history of one day was that of all,"[7] James Williams wrote. Frederick Douglass, a slave in Maryland before he escaped in 1838 to become a well-known antislavery spokesman, remembered, "It was never too hot or too cold; it could never rain, blow hail, or snow, too hard for us to work in the field. Work, work, work, was scarcely more the order of the day than of the night."[8]

CHAPTER TWO

Slaves in the Big House

Not all plantation slaves labored in the fields. Some worked in the plantation owner's home. Large or small, built of logs or bricks, this home was known as the "Big House." Slaves in the Big House were required to serve the needs, wants, meals, and activities of the white people who lived there.

Like the field hands, house slaves rose before sunup and were on duty until late at night. Although working in the house was more comfortable than in the fields, house slaves often had less time to themselves than field hands. Out in the vast fields, the master could not watch every field hand every moment of the day. But house slaves were almost constantly under the watchful eye of the lady of the house, called the **mistress**, and on call to do whatever she assigned. Some house slaves had to sleep in the kitchen—unable to retreat to a private place of their own even at night.

Women's Work

Much of the work of the Big House was divided between men and women. Women worked as cooks to prepare

A slave family stands before the master and mistress of the Big House. Slaves who worked in the plantation owner's home were known as house slaves.

the plantation family's meals, and sometimes also the slaves' meals. They served as maids to clean house and attend to the mistress's personal needs. They washed laundry and cared for the planter's children.

The cook held one of the most important positions. She was in charge of the kitchen, a separate building next to the Big House. Nothing about cooking was quick or easy in plantation days. Every morning the fire had to be

built and stoked. Dried corn kernels were ground into grits and boiled over a flame. Biscuits were mixed and beaten by hand, and then baked. Starting hours before sunrise, the cook could have a breakfast of biscuits, gravy thickened with lard and cornstarch, grits, and coffee ready for the plantation family members by seven o'clock.

House slaves served the family their meals in the dining room. When the family finished eating, the cook and other house slaves usually were allowed to eat the leftovers back in the kitchen. After this quick meal it was time to clean up from breakfast—and start on the next meal, the midday dinner, only a few hours away.

The cook was an important worker in the Big House, but she could never forget that she was a slave. The master and mistress might praise her work, but they might as easily criticize it. Harriet Jacobs, who was a slave in North Carolina, had a demanding mistress. "If dinner was not served at the exact time on . . . Sunday," Jacobs wrote, "she would station herself in the kitchen, and wait till it was dished, and then spit in all the kettles and pans that had been used for cooking."[9] The mistress did this to prevent the cook and her children from enjoying the pan scrapings and gravy as leftovers.

The work of the maids brought them in close contact with the slave owner's family. Early in the morning, the personal maid to the plantation's mistress heated water over a fire and brought it to her bedchamber. This usually required climbing a flight of stairs while balancing a heavy cauldron of hot water. The maid had to make sure the mistress had sufficient soap and towels at hand for her morning washup. She also helped the mistress arrange her hair and get dressed. Nursemaids performed similar services for the plantation owners' children.

Other housemaids were responsible for cleaning the Big House. They swept floors, and got down on their hands and knees to polish the wood with wax. There was no indoor plumbing with running water and toilets, so the housemaids emptied washbasins and cleaned out chamber pots. They dusted furniture. Julia Frazer, who as a girl was a house slave in Virginia, preferred dusting to her other duties. When she cleaned her owner's library, sometimes she explored the books, lingering over one in particular that had pictures of kings and queens—people who were free.

The laundress had one of the most strenuous jobs in the Big House. First she had to sort the clothes and soak very dirty items overnight in cold water. Next she needed to boil kettles of water over a wood fire. She washed the laundry in the boiling hot water, sometimes changing the water several times before the clothes rinsed clean. The weekly load of laundry might take more than four hundred pounds of water—all of which had to be hauled

Some female slaves served as nursemaids. They were responsible for taking care of the plantation owners' children.

from one place to another. There were no faucets or washing machines.

Men of the Big House

Although men sometimes worked as cooks and cleaners in the Big House, they usually had other jobs. Large plantations had a butler, a slave who was responsible for the general operation of the household. Another slave served as valet to the plantation owner, taking care of his personal bathing and dressing needs. Coachmen took care of the owner's horse-drawn carriage, as well as the horses.

Some very large plantations were like small villages. Nearly everything needed by the plantation inhabitants

Some male slaves served as butlers. They were responsible for the overall operation of the household.

A slave boy serves drinks to his master and guests. Slave children worked in the Big House until they were old enough to work in the fields.

was produced right on the plantation, even furniture, leather goods, and metalware. On these plantations, certain male slaves had skilled jobs. They worked as carpenters, crafting wood furniture and cabinets. Cobblers produced leather shoes. Blacksmiths forged horseshoes, fences, and gates out of iron.

Jobs for Children

Boys and girls worked in the Big House as well. Young male slaves worked as "yard boys" to keep the grounds raked and tended. They ran errands for the master or mistress. Other children cleaned, washed dishes, and looked after babies. They carried water to slaves working in the fields—where they would work before long.

But before they got sent out to work in the fields, the child slaves of the Big House might be required to do pretty much anything their owners desired—including things that seem strange. When he was seven years old, James Monroe Abbot's job was to stand at his owner's bedside to shoo away the flies. Henry Bibb of Tennessee had a slightly different assignment. "She [the mistress] was too lazy to scratch her own head," he wrote, "and would often make me scratch and comb it for her." [10] William Mathews of Louisiana had another task. "I was what they called the 'waiting boy,'" he explained. "I sat in that buggy and wait till they come out of where they was. I wasn't allowed to visit 'round with the other slaves. No sir, I had to set there and wait." [11]

If some of the jobs that child slaves had to do were foolish, others were frightening. George Briggs was a slave in South Carolina. As a boy, one of his jobs was to cut branches from hickory trees. The branches were made into broom handles. They were also made into whips. As all slaves knew, whether they worked in the Big House or in the field, doing a good job was not going to earn them money. But doing a poor job could easily earn them a whipping—a whipping made possible, and painful, by the good work of a young boy who cut branches from hickory trees.

CHAPTER THREE

Home Life

Plantation owners viewed slaves as property. Slaves were the same as tools or plow horses. No matter what slaveholders thought, however, slaves were human beings. They fell in love, married, and had children. They tried to turn their rough cabins into family homes. Slave owners held such tight control over the slaves' lives—regulating everything from whom they married to where they slept—that slaves faced tremendous barriers to creating families and homes. Still, they never stopped trying.

"Now You're Married"

Despite long hours of work, young slave men and women found ways to meet. On Saturday nights, slaves were allowed time to themselves. That was when slaves from different plantations got together to dance, play music, and eat. They also spent time with one another on Sundays, when they were permitted to attend Christian church services.

When two slaves on the same plantation wanted to get married, they had to get the permission of their master. If they were from two different plantations, both masters had to agree. A slave marriage ceremony was an informal affair. "Now you're married," the slaveholder would say, and the slaves would be married.

Married couples on the same plantation were able to live together. If a husband and wife were from different plantations, they had to continue living apart. On Saturday nights and Sundays, the husband would stay with his wife on her plantation. Slave children usually stayed with their mothers.

Slaves participate in a wedding celebration. Slaves needed their masters' permission to get married.

Slave Quarters

In some ways all slave **quarters** on all plantations were the same. The wooden cabins or huts that made up the quarters were built away from the Big House. They were small, plain, and rough. In summer they were hot, and in winter they were cold.

Some plantation owners provided better quarters, and some worse. The better cabins were constructed of logs or other framing covered with clapboard to keep out wind and rain. They had wood floors, glass windows, a door that opened and closed securely, and a fireplace.

But most slave quarters did not meet even these low standards. Throughout the South, plantation slaves had to live in log cabins with dirt floors, leaky roofs, drafty walls, and no real windows. The door was a hole in the wall. A family or a group of unmarried slaves shared a single room, approximately twelve or fourteen feet square. "We had old ragged huts made out of poles,"[12] recalled Jenny Proctor, who was a slave in Alabama. On the North Carolina plantation where Allen Parker was enslaved, the huts had windows, but no glass. "The windows had only wooden shutters

Most slaves lived in poorly built wooden cabins located away from the Big House.

which could be closed when desired," he recalled, "but this would of course leave the cabin in darkness."[13]

Inside a slave cabin, there was little furniture. Instead of a real bed, most slaves had a platform fastened to the wall. They also might have a simple wooden table and some benches. House slaves or the master's or mistress's favorites sometimes received cast-off furniture and dishes that the plantation owners no longer wanted. Other slaves crafted their own furnishings to make their crude huts more like a home. They made tables and chairs from wood and other materials. They carved plates out of wood and made bowls out of gourds. Sometimes their handicrafts reflected the designs and decorations of their ancestors' African homelands.

Coarse Clothing

Along with home furnishings, hand-me-down clothing from plantation owners was sometimes given to favored house slaves. But most slaves had only the barest wardrobe. To save money, owners gave slaves the fewest possible items of clothing. On some plantations, a slave received one set of clothing per year, at Christmas. When these wore out, the slaves could not obtain replacements. Other slave owners might give up to four sets.

Men wore shirts and pants of rough homespun cotton, with wool pants in the winter. Women wore long skirts and blouses, also of cotton or wool. Much of the clothing came from northern factories, which made cheap, rough cloth especially for southern slaveholders. Men and women wore leather shoes, although the shoes were generally so uncomfortable that slaves often went barefoot.

As for children, "Boys and gals all dressed just alike, one long shirt or dress," said Abram Sells, who lived on a plantation in Texas. "They call it a shirt if a boy wear it and call it a dress if the gal wear it." [14] Children received no shoes. Unless another slave made them shoes, they went barefoot in every season.

Slave women wore long skirts and blouses made of cotton or wool. Most slaves had very few pieces of clothing.

A slave accompanies her mistress to the market.

Their Daily Cornbread

Plantation owners were usually as stingy about the food they gave their slaves as they were about clothing. The mainstay of the slaves' diet was cornmeal, as well as some kind of hog meat, either bacon or salt pork. Cornmeal was boiled with water into mush. It was also cooked over hot coals or baked into loaves. This cornbread was called john-nycake, but on the Mississippi plantation where Louis

Hughes was enslaved, the slaves had a different name for it. "Their daily food was corn bread," he wrote, "which they called 'Johnny Constant,' as they had it constantly." [15]

The amount of food slaveholders provided an adult slave each week was around a **peck,** or eight quarts, of cornmeal and two to four pounds of pork or bacon. Food was usually handed out once a week, typically on Saturday evening. On many plantations, it was up to the slaves to prepare their meals. Because they rose so early in the morning, field hands had only a small breakfast on the run—cornbread or mush and bacon—if they ate at all.

If they had to eat in the fields, they packed more of the same in a bucket. At night the slaves cooked their meals over a fire in their cabins' fireplaces. If their owners gave them iron pans, they would fry bacon and cornmeal cakes. If not, the slaves would put their food directly in the fire to cook, and scrape the ashes off to eat it when it was done.

On some plantations, slaves did not cook their own meals in their cabins, but instead ate meals prepared by slave cooks. Young children also were fed as a group, while their parents toiled in the fields. Frequently the plantation owner or mistress fed them as if they were little animals. Frederick Douglass recalled, "Our food was coarse corn meal boiled. This was called *mush*. It was put into a large wooden tray or trough, and set down upon the ground. The children were then called, like so many pigs, and like so many pigs they would come and devour the mush; some with oyster-shells, others with pieces of shingle, some with naked hands, and none with spoons."[16]

The quality of a plantation slave's diet depended greatly on the plantation owner. Some owners regularly

A plantation owner and his family visit the slave quarters.

provided vegetables, meat, and fruit in addition to the usual cornmeal and bacon. Some allowed their slaves to grow their own vegetables in little gardens called "patches." In addition many slaves hunted and fished. On Saturday nights women tried to cook something special for their families, such as opossum, raccoon, or fish. With those dishes they might prepare hopping John—rice and black-eyed peas—or collard greens and squash from their gardens. Slaves tried to make foods that had more flavor than their boring everyday fare, using red peppers and vinegar, and cooking up barbecue and gumbo.

Day after day, slaves strained and sweated to raise farm products. And yet, although surrounded by food, many ate poorly. They were well aware of the unfairness of their situation. As one slave song put it:

> *We raise the wheat,*
> *They give us the corn;*
> *We bake the bread,*
> *They give us the crust;*
> *We sift the meal,*
> *They give us the husk;*
> *We peel the meat,*
> *They give us the skin;*
> *And that's the way*
> *They take us in.* [17]

CHAPTER FOUR

Times of Sorrow

B esides long days of unpaid labor, poor housing, skimpy clothes, and monotonous food, plantation slaves endured even worse ordeals. On a daily basis, they faced the threat of painful punishments if they behaved in a manner that the master or overseer did not like. They also knew that, at any time, the plantation owner could sell them or members of their family to another slaveholder, and that they might never see the people they loved again.

Power of the Whip

How often and how severely a slave was punished depended on the plantation owner and overseer. The most common punishment was whipping, also known as flogging. Masters used a variety of flogging tools. Besides ordinary cowhide whips, some favored heavier bullwhips, made of braided **rawhide** with a knot at the end. Switches, whips made of flexible tree branches, were also used.

Even a single lash from one of these whips stung, but a whipping was not limited to a single lash. A field hand who did not pick enough cotton to satisfy the overseer might receive forty lashes. For picking dirty cotton, a slave might get twenty lashes. A house slave who served a burned biscuit, or a slave who was late leaving his cabin at daybreak, faced similar punishments.

Before they were whipped, slaves had to strip off their clothes. They were tied to a tree or post. During whippings, the lashes cut into the slaves' bare skin, usually on their backs. Often, owners or overseers poured saltwater over the open wounds, which increased the torment.

Field hands who did not pick enough cotton would often be whipped.

An overseer watches as one slave whips another. Overseers and owners often forced slaves to whip each other.

The power to punish brought out a cruel streak in many plantation owners and overseers. Sarah Douglas's owner ensured that her whippings would be especially painful by tying a nugget of lead to the end of the cowhide whip. The mistress of the South Carolina plantation where John Andrew Jackson was enslaved took the lead in whipping the house slaves. "She would tie the female slaves, who did the domestic work, to trees or bedposts, whichever was handiest," Jackson wrote, "and whip them severely with a dogwood or hickory switch, for the slightest offence, and often for nothing at all apparently, but merely for the purpose of keeping up her practice." [18]

Creative Cruelty

Some punishments were meant to treat the slave as less than human. A slave who stole food from the plantation owner's storage rooms, for example, might have to wear an iron collar with bells on it. Like a cowbell around the neck of a cow, the collar alerted everyone to the slave's movements. Some slave owners chose to embarrass male slaves for disobedience by forcing them to wear women's clothing.

Punishments frequently were designed to deprive slaves of their meager privileges. Withholding food, especially meat, from a slave was a common penalty. Owners also took away food that slaves grew in their little gardens, and required slaves to work on Sundays to punish them. Still other punishments were more cruelly creative. On tobacco plantations, slaves who failed to find and remove the worms that infested tobacco leaves were sometimes forced to eat them.

Not all slaves had to endure beatings or other violent punishments. Some plantation owners believed that whippings were inhumane. Others did not flog slaves because they wanted them to appear healthy and content—the sort of slaves who would bring a good price at the slave market.

Families Divided

The most dreaded event in the life of most plantation slaves was a slave market or auction. Harsh as their lives were, slaves made friends, families, and homes on their plantations. They lost all these comforts when they were sold and forced to move away with a new slave owner.

Slaves had no power to prevent owners from splitting up their families through sales to different buyers. When Charles Ball was a very young boy in Maryland, the master of the plantation where he and his mother were enslaved died. Ball was sold to another Maryland slaveholder. His mother was sold to a Georgia slave

Slaves dreaded slave auctions and markets because they might be separated from their families.

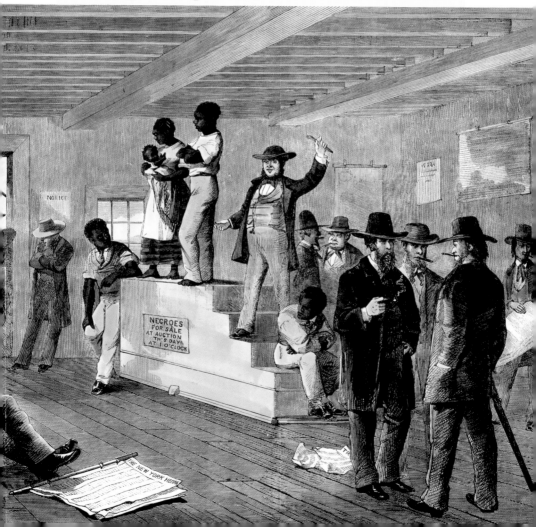

trader. When the young boy's new owner started to ride away with Ball on his horse, Ball's mother ran after him. She begged the white man to buy her, too. When her own new master saw what was happening, he came after her with a rawhide whip and dragged her away. "My master then quickened the pace of his horse," Ball wrote, "and as we advanced, the cries of my poor parent became more and more indistinct—at length they died away in the distance, and I never again heard the voice of my poor mother." [19]

Risky Escapes

For some slaves, being wrenched from family and friends by a sale and relocation was the last straw. Of all the reasons slaves had for trying to escape from their plantations, this separation gave many the courage to risk running away. The risks were serious for runaways. The countryside was full of snakes and other harmful wildlife. Obtaining food on the run was a problem. But the greatest danger of all was a white man with a dog.

When a slave was missing on a plantation, word was sent to nearby plantations. The plantation owner pressured other slaves to tell what they knew about the missing person's whereabouts. Then the owner sent out search parties, complete with bloodhounds. Some hired professional slave catchers, who had packs of hounds specially trained to track down slaves.

Dogs were frequently successful in hunting down runaway slaves. They were known to attack their human prey, sometimes viciously. Hounds killed a slave known as Little John, who tried to run away from the same Alabama

A female slave cries out after she is sold to a new owner. Many slaves ran away after being separated from their families.

plantation where James Williams was enslaved. "The murdered young man had a mother and two sisters on the plantation, by whom he was dearly loved," wrote Williams. "When I told the old woman of what had befallen her son, she only said that it was better for poor John than to live in slavery."[20]

Had he lived, Little John would have suffered severe punishment for his attempt to escape. After the punishment, he could have looked forward to more toil, hardship, humiliation, and sorrow—just the usual routine for a plantation slave. Little John's mother might be forgiven for saying that her son was better off dead.

But in slaves, as in all human beings, the will to live was strong. The enslaved men, women, and children of America's southern plantations survived. They worked and developed skills. Against all odds, they created loving families and homes. Slaveholders and society treated them as less than human—but the slaves' lives and ability to survive showed just how human they were.

Notes

Chapter One: Working the Fields

1. James Williams, *Narrative of James Williams, an American Slave, Who Was for Several Years a Driver on a Cotton Plantation in Alabama.* New York: American Anti-Slavery Society, 1838, at University of North Carolina at Chapel Hill Libraries, Documenting the American South. http://docsouth.unc.edu.
2. Quoted in B.A. Botkin, ed., *Lay My Burden Down: A Folk History of Slavery.* New York: Delta, 1973, p. 121.
3. Louis Hughes, *Thirty Years a Slave.* Milwaukee: South Side Printing, 1897, at University of North Carolina at Chapel Hill Libraries. Documenting the American South. http://docsouth.unc.edu.
4. Mary Reynolds, *WPA Slave Narrative Project,* vol. 16, part 3, *Texas Narratives,* at Library of Congress, Born in Slavery: Slave Narratives from the Federal Writers' Project, 1936–1938. http://memory.loc.gov.
5. John Andrew Jackson, *The Experience of a Slave in South Carolina.* London: Passmore & Alabaster, 1862, at University of North Carolina at Chapel Hill Libraries. Documenting the American South. http://docsouth.unc.edu.
6. Quoted in Belinda Hurmence, *Slavery Time When I Was Chillun.* New York: Putnam's, 1997, pp. 34–35.
7. Williams, *Narrative of James Williams.*
8. Quoted in Wilma King, *Stolen Childhood: Slave Youth in Nineteenth-Century America.* Bloomington & Indianapolis: Indianapolis University Press, 1995, p. 21.

Chapter Two: Slaves in the Big House

9. Harriet Jacobs, *Incidents in the Life of a Slave Girl.* New York: Signet Classic, 2000, p. 10.

10. Quoted in King, *Stolen Childhood,* p. 26.

11. Quoted in Hurmence, *Slavery Time,* p. 3.

Chapter Three: Home Life

12. Quoted in Botkin, *Lay My Burden Down,* p. 99.

13. Allen Parker, *Recollection of Slavery Times.* Worcester, MA: Chas. W. Burbank, 1895, at East Carolina University, The Allen Parker Slave Narrative Project, 2000. http://core.ecu.edu.

14. Quoted in Hurmence, *Slavery Time,* p. 28.

15. Hughes, *Thirty Years a Slave.*

16. Frederick Douglass, *Narrative of the Life of Frederick Douglass, an American Slave.* Boston: The Anti-Slavery Office, 1845, at University of North Carolina at Chapel Hill Libraries, Documenting the American South. http://docsouth.unc.edu.

17. Quoted in King, *Stolen Childhood,* p. 37.

Chapter Four: Times of Sorrow

18. Jackson, *The Experience of a Slave in South Carolina.*

19. Charles Ball, *Fifty Years in Chains; or, the Life of an American Slave.* New York: H. Dayton, 1859, at University of North Carolina at Chapel Hill Libraries, Documenting the American South. http://docsouth.unc.edu.

20. Williams, *Narrative of James Williams.*

Glossary

driver: A plantation slave who is in charge of a gang or group of other slaves in the field.

field hand: A slave who works in the fields on a plantation to plant, tend, and harvest crops.

harvest: The time or season when ripe crops are gathered for use or sale.

master: A male slave owner.

mistress: The wife of a slave owner, or a female slave owner.

overseer: A person hired by a plantation owner to supervise the field hands.

peck: A quantity, equal to about eight quarts, used to measure dry food such as cornmeal.

plantation: A large farm or estate where crops are raised.

quarters: A place where people live, such as the slave quarters on a plantation.

rawhide: The skin or hide of cattle, which was made into whips during plantation days.

For Further Exploration

Books

Raymond Bial, *The Strength of These Arms*. New York: Houghton Mifflin, 1997. With photographs from plantation sites and quotations from slaves and their descendants, this book tells about the work, meals, family life, and sufferings of slaves.

Paul Erickson, *Daily Life on a Southern Plantation, 1853*. New York: Lodestar, 1998. This volume is illustrated with photographs of Shadows-on-the-Teche, a nine-hundred-acre Louisiana sugarcane plantation built in the 1830s, which is now a museum. Life in the Big House and in the slave quarters is depicted.

Bobbie Kalman, *Life on a Plantation*. New York: Crabtree, 1997. This large-format book includes color pictures and photographs from plantations that have been restored, including a plantation in Colonial Williamsburg.

Julius Lester, *To Be a Slave*. New York: Puffin, 1968. This Newberry Honor Book includes quotations from slave narratives, along with the author's explanation of the life of a slave from capture in Africa to freedom at the end of the Civil War.

Patricia C. McKissack and Frederick L. McKissack, *Christmas in the Big House, Christmas in the Quarters*. New York: Scholastic, 1994. The Christmas holiday season on a plantation is the subject of this book, which discusses both the traditions of slaves and plantation owners.

Websites

Library of Congress, Born in Slavery: Slave Narratives from the Federal Writers' Project, 1936–1938 (http://memory.loc.gov/ammem/snhtml). The Library of Congress has put online more than two thousand interviews with former slaves conducted during the 1930s. The website also includes hundreds of photographs of former slaves.

University of North Carolina at Chapel Hill Libraries, Documenting the American South, North American Slave Narratives (http://docsouth.unc.edu/neh/neh.html). This university library site includes more than two hundred texts in which slaves tell their own stories.

Index

Picture Credits

Cover image: Bridgeman Art Library

© Bettmann/CORBIS, 14–15

© Hulton/Archive by Getty Images, 22–23

Chris Jouan, 5, 6

© North Wind Picture Archives, 7, 9, 11, 17, 18, 19, 24, 26, 27, 28–29, 32, 33, 37

About the Author

Debbie Levy's *Slaves on a Southern Plantation* is her eighth nonfiction book for children. Her earlier books include *Maryland*, published by KidHaven Press in 2003, and books on civil liberties, bigotry, and medical ethics for KidHaven's sister press, Lucent Books. Levy earned a bachelor's degree in government and foreign affairs from the University of Virginia, as well as a law degree and a master's degree in world politics from the University of Michigan. She practiced law with a large Washington, D.C., law firm and worked as a newspaper editor. Levy enjoys paddling around in kayaks and canoes and fishing in the Chesapeake Bay region. She lives with her husband and their two sons in Maryland.